Especially For

From

Date

A Mother's Daily Prayer

•JOURNAL•

BARBOUR
PUBLISHING

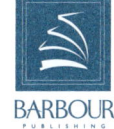

© 2014 by Barbour Publishing, Inc.

Compiled by Kathy Shutt.

ISBN 978-1-62416-830-7/ A Mother's Daily Prayer Journal
ISBN 978-1-62416-832-1/ A Father's Daily Prayer Journal
ISBN 978-1-62416-831-4/ A Grad's Daily Prayer Journal

All rights reserved. No part of this publication may be reproduced or transmitted for commercial purposes, except for brief quotations in printed reviews, without written permission of the publisher.

Scripture quotations marked KJV are taken from the King James Version of the Bible.

Scripture quotations marked NIV are taken from the HOLY BIBLE, NEW INTERNATIONAL VERSION®. NIV®. Copyright © 1973, 1978, 1984, 2011 by Biblica, Inc.™ Used by permission. All rights reserved worldwide.

Scripture quotations marked MSG are from *THE MESSAGE*. Copyright © by Eugene H. Peterson 1993, 1994, 1995, 1996, 2000, 2001, 2002. Used by permission of NavPress Publishing Group.

Scripture quotations marked NLT are taken from the Holy Bible. New Living Translation copyright© 1996, 2004, 2007 by Tyndale House Foundation. Used by permission of Tyndale House Publishers, Inc. Carol Stream, Illinois 60188. All rights reserved.

Scripture quotations marked NKJV are taken from the New King James Version®. Copyright © 1982 by Thomas Nelson, Inc. Used by permission. All rights reserved.

Scripture quotations marked NASB are taken from the New American Standard Bible, © 1960, 1962, 1963, 1968, 1971, 1972, 1973, 1975, 1977, 1995 by The Lockman Foundation. Used by permission.

Scripture quotations marked NRSV are taken from the New Revised Standard Version Bible, copyright 1989, Division of Christian Education of the National Council of the Churches of Christ in the United States of America. Used by permission. All rights reserved.

Scripture taken from the Good News Translation® (Today's English Standard Version, Second Edition), Copyright © 1992 American Bible Society. All rights reserved.

Published by Barbour Publishing, Inc., P.O. Box 719, Uhrichsville, Ohio 44683, www.barbourbooks.com

Our mission is to publish and distribute inspirational products offering exceptional value and biblical encouragement to the masses.

Printed in China.

*Evening and morning and at noon
I will pray, and cry aloud,
And He shall hear my voice.*
Psalm 55:17 nkjv

Day 1

Today's Date:
Prayer Requests and Answers to Prayer

My Thoughts and Praises

> *We give thanks to God and the Father of our Lord Jesus Christ, praying always for you.*
> Colossians 1:3 kjv

Day 2

Today's Date:
Prayer Requests and Answers to Prayer

My Thoughts and Praises

Day 3

Today's Date:
Prayer Requests and Answers to Prayer

My Thoughts and Praises

Day 4

Today's Date:
Prayer Requests and Answers to Prayer

My Thoughts and Praises

Day 5

Today's Date:
Prayer Requests and Answers to Prayer

My Thoughts and Praises

Day 6

Today's Date:
Prayer Requests and Answers to Prayer

My Thoughts and Praises

Day 7

Today's Date:
Prayer Requests and Answers to Prayer

My Thoughts and Praises

> *Prayer is not conquering God's reluctance,
> but taking hold of God's willingness.*
> PHILLIPS BROOKS

Day 8

Today's Date:
Prayer Requests and Answers to Prayer

My Thoughts and Praises

Day 9

Today's Date:
Prayer Requests and Answers to Prayer

My Thoughts and Praises

> *But when you pray, go into your room, close the door and pray to your Father, who is unseen. Then your Father, who sees what is done in secret, will reward you.*
> MATTHEW 6:6 NIV

Day 10

Today's Date:
Prayer Requests and Answers to Prayer

My Thoughts and Praises

Day 11

Today's Date:
Prayer Requests and Answers to Prayer

My Thoughts and Praises

Day 12

Today's Date:
Prayer Requests and Answers to Prayer

My Thoughts and Praises

Day 13

Today's Date:
Prayer Requests and Answers to Prayer

My Thoughts and Praises

Day 14

Today's Date:
Prayer Requests and Answers to Prayer

My Thoughts and Praises

Day 15

Today's Date:

Prayer Requests and Answers to Prayer

My Thoughts and Praises

> *God shapes the world by prayer. The more prayer there is in the world the better the world will be, the mightier the forces against evil....*
> E. M. BOUNDS

Day 16

Today's Date:

Prayer Requests and Answers to Prayer

My Thoughts and Praises

Day 17

Today's Date:
Prayer Requests and Answers to Prayer

My Thoughts and Praises

> *Pray in the Holy Spirit;*
> *keep yourselves in the love of God.*
> JUDE 20–21 NRSV

Day 18

Today's Date:
Prayer Requests and Answers to Prayer

My Thoughts and Praises

Day 19

Today's Date:
Prayer Requests and Answers to Prayer

My Thoughts and Praises

Day 20

Today's Date:
Prayer Requests and Answers to Prayer

My Thoughts and Praises

Day 21

Today's Date:
Prayer Requests and Answers to Prayer

My Thoughts and Praises

Day 22

Today's Date:
Prayer Requests and Answers to Prayer

My Thoughts and Praises

Day 23

Today's Date:
Prayer Requests and Answers to Prayer

My Thoughts and Praises

> *Don't pray when you feel like it.*
> *Have an appointment with the Lord and keep it.*
> *A man is powerful on his knees.*
> CORRIE TEN BOOM

Day 24

Today's Date:
Prayer Requests and Answers to Prayer

My Thoughts and Praises

Day 25

Today's Date:
Prayer Requests and Answers to Prayer

My Thoughts and Praise

> *For. . .we don't know what God wants us to pray for. But the Holy Spirit prays for us with groanings that cannot be expressed in words.*
> ROMANS 8:26 NLT

Day 26

Today's Date:
Prayer Requests and Answers to Prayer

My Thoughts and Praises

Day 27

Today's Date:
Prayer Requests and Answers to Prayer

My Thoughts and Praises

Day 28

Today's Date:
Prayer Requests and Answers to Prayer

My Thoughts and Praises

Day 29

Today's Date:
Prayer Requests and Answers to Prayer

My Thoughts and Praises

Day 30

Today's Date:
Prayer Requests and Answers to Prayer

My Thoughts and Praises

Day 31

Today's Date:
Prayer Requests and Answers to Prayer

My Thoughts and Praises

> *Satan trembles when he sees the weakest Christian on his knees.*
> — WILLIAM COWPER

Day 32

Today's Date:
Prayer Requests and Answers to Prayer

My Thoughts and Praises

Day 33

Today's Date:
Prayer Requests and Answers to Prayer

My Thoughts and Praises

> *I pray that the eyes of your heart may be enlightened in order that you may know the hope to which he has called you, the riches of his glorious inheritance. . .*
> EPHESIANS 1:18 NIV

Day 34

Today's Date:
Prayer Requests and Answers to Prayer

My Thoughts and Praises

Day 35

Today's Date:
Prayer Requests and Answers to Prayer

My Thoughts and Praises

Day 36

Today's Date:
Prayer Requests and Answers to Prayer

My Thoughts and Praises

Day 37

Today's Date:
Prayer Requests and Answers to Prayer

My Thoughts and Praises

Day 38

Today's Date:
Prayer Requests and Answers to Prayer

My Thoughts and Praises

Day 39

Today's Date: ....
Prayer Requests and Answers to Prayer ....

....
....
....
....

My Thoughts and Praises ....

....
....
....
....

> *He who has learned to pray has learned the greatest secret of a holy and happy life.*
> — WILLIAM LAW

Day 40

Today's Date: ....
Prayer Requests and Answers to Prayer ....

....
....
....
....

My Thoughts and Praises ....

....
....
....
....

Day 41

Today's Date:
Prayer Requests and Answers to Prayer

My Thoughts and Praises

> *They that wait upon the Lord shall renew their strength; they shall mount up with wings as eagles; they shall run, and not be weary; and they shall walk, and not faint.*
> Isaiah 40:31 kjv

Day 42

Today's Date:
Prayer Requests and Answers to Prayer

My Thoughts and Praises

Day 43

Today's Date:
Prayer Requests and Answers to Prayer

My Thoughts and Praises

Day 44

Today's Date:
Prayer Requests and Answers to Prayer

My Thoughts and Praises

Day 45

Today's Date:
Prayer Requests and Answers to Prayer

My Thoughts and Praises

Day 46

Today's Date:
Prayer Requests and Answers to Prayer

My Thoughts and Praises

Day 47

Today's Date:
Prayer Requests and Answers to Prayer

My Thoughts and Praises

> *We have to pray with our eyes on God, not on the difficulties.*
> OSWALD CHAMBERS

Day 48

Today's Date:
Prayer Requests and Answers to Prayer

My Thoughts and Praises

Day 49

Today's Date:
Prayer Requests and Answers to Prayer

My Thoughts and Praises

Come to me, all you who labor and are heavy laden, and I will give you rest.
MATTHEW 11:28 NKJV

Day 50

Today's Date:
Prayer Requests and Answers to Prayer

My Thoughts and Praises

Day 51

Today's Date:
Prayer Requests and Answers to Prayer

My Thoughts and Praises

Day 52

Today's Date:
Prayer Requests and Answers to Prayer

My Thoughts and Praises

Day 53

Today's Date:
Prayer Requests and Answers to Prayer

My Thoughts and Praises

Day 54

Today's Date:
Prayer Requests and Answers to Prayer

My Thoughts and Praises

Day 55

Today's Date:

Prayer Requests and Answers to Prayer

My Thoughts and Praises

> *As is the business of tailors to make clothes and cobblers to make shoes, so it is the business of Christians to pray.*
> MARTIN LUTHER

Day 56

Today's Date:

Prayer Requests and Answers to Prayer

My Thoughts and Praises

Day 57

Today's Date:
Prayer Requests and Answers to Prayer

My Thoughts and Praises

> *"If you remain in me and my words remain in you, ask whatever you wish, and it will be done for you."*
> JOHN 15:7 NIV

Day 58

Today's Date:
Prayer Requests and Answers to Prayer

My Thoughts and Praises

Day 59

Today's Date:
Prayer Requests and Answers to Prayer

My Thoughts and Praises

Day 60

Today's Date:
Prayer Requests and Answers to Prayer

My Thoughts and Praises

Day 61

Today's Date:
Prayer Requests and Answers to Prayer

My Thoughts and Praises

Day 62

Today's Date:
Prayer Requests and Answers to Prayer

My Thoughts and Praises

Day 63

Today's Date:
Prayer Requests and Answers to Prayer

My Thoughts and Praises

> *Prayer does not fit us for the greater work;
> prayer is the greater work.*
> OSWALD CHAMBERS

Day 64

Today's Date:
Prayer Requests and Answers to Prayer

My Thoughts and Praises

Day 65

Today's Date:
Prayer Requests and Answers to Prayer

My Thoughts and Praises

> *You, God, are my God,*
> *earnestly I seek you.*
> Psalm 63:1 niv

Day 66

Today's Date:
Prayer Requests and Answers to Prayer

My Thoughts and Praises

Day 67

Today's Date:
Prayer Requests and Answers to Prayer

My Thoughts and Praises

Day 68

Today's Date:
Prayer Requests and Answers to Prayer

My Thoughts and Praises

Day 69

Today's Date:

Prayer Requests and Answers to Prayer

My Thoughts and Praises

Day 70

Today's Date:

Prayer Requests and Answers to Prayer

My Thoughts and Praises

Day 71

Today's Date:
Prayer Requests and Answers to Prayer

My Thoughts and Praises

Prayer can never be in excess.
C. H. Spurgeon

Day 72

Today's Date:
Prayer Requests and Answers to Prayer

My Thoughts and Praises

Day 73

Today's Date:
Prayer Requests and Answers to Prayer

My Thoughts and Praises

> *"Lord, teach us to pray."*
> Luke 11:1 niv

Day 74

Today's Date:
Prayer Requests and Answers to Prayer

My Thoughts and Praises

Day 75

Today's Date:
Prayer Requests and Answers to Prayer

My Thoughts and Praises

Day 76

Today's Date:
Prayer Requests and Answers to Prayer

My Thoughts and Praises

Day 77

Today's Date:
Prayer Requests and Answers to Prayer

My Thoughts and Praises

Day 78

Today's Date:
Prayer Requests and Answers to Prayer

My Thoughts and Praises

Day 79

Today's Date:
Prayer Requests and Answers to Prayer

My Thoughts and Praises

The wings of prayer can carry high and far.
UNKNOWN

Day 80

Today's Date:
Prayer Requests and Answers to Prayer

My Thoughts and Praises

Day 81

Today's Date:
Prayer Requests and Answers to Prayer

My Thoughts and Praises

Let the peace that comes from Christ rule in your hearts.
COLOSSIANS 3:15 NLT

Day 82

Today's Date:
Prayer Requests and Answers to Prayer

My Thoughts and Praises

Day 83

Today's Date:
Prayer Requests and Answers to Prayer

My Thoughts and Praises

Day 84

Today's Date:
Prayer Requests and Answers to Prayer

My Thoughts and Praises

Day 85

Today's Date:
Prayer Requests and Answers to Prayer

My Thoughts and Praises

Day 86

Today's Date:
Prayer Requests and Answers to Prayer

My Thoughts and Praises

Day 87

Today's Date:
Prayer Requests and Answers to Prayer

My Thoughts and Praises

> *Prayer—secret, fervent, believing prayer—
> lies at the root of all personal godliness.*
> WILLIAM CAREY

Day 88

Today's Date:
Prayer Requests and Answers to Prayer

My Thoughts and Praises

Day 89

Today's Date:
Prayer Requests and Answers to Prayer

My Thoughts and Praises

> *May these words of my mouth and this meditation of my heart be pleasing in your sight.*
> PSALM 19:14 NIV

Day 90

Today's Date:
Prayer Requests and Answers to Prayer

My Thoughts and Praises

Day 91

Today's Date:
Prayer Requests and Answers to Prayer

My Thoughts and Praises

Day 92

Today's Date:
Prayer Requests and Answers to Prayer

My Thoughts and Praises

Day 93

Today's Date:
Prayer Requests and Answers to Prayer

My Thoughts and Praises

Day 94

Today's Date:
Prayer Requests and Answers to Prayer

My Thoughts and Praises

Day 95

Today's Date:
Prayer Requests and Answers to Prayer

My Thoughts and Praises

> *Ten minutes spent in the presence of Christ every day...*
> *will make the whole day different.*
> HENRY DRUMMOND

Day 96

Today's Date:
Prayer Requests and Answers to Prayer

My Thoughts and Praises

Day 97

Today's Date:
Prayer Requests and Answers to Prayer

My Thoughts and Praises

Whether you turn to the right or to the left, your ears will hear a voice behind you, saying, "This is the way; walk in it."
Isaiah 30:21 niv

Day 98

Today's Date:
Prayer Requests and Answers to Prayer

My Thoughts and Praises

Day 99

Today's Date:
Prayer Requests and Answers to Prayer

My Thoughts and Praises

Day 100

Today's Date:
Prayer Requests and Answers to Prayer

My Thoughts and Praises

Day 101

Today's Date:
Prayer Requests and Answers to Prayer

My Thoughts and Praises

Day 102

Today's Date:
Prayer Requests and Answers to Prayer

My Thoughts and Praises

Day 103

Today's Date:
Prayer Requests and Answers to Prayer

My Thoughts and Praises

> *There has never been a spiritual awakening in any country or locality that did not begin in united prayer.*
> A. T. Pierson

Day 104

Today's Date:
Prayer Requests and Answers to Prayer

My Thoughts and Praises

Day 105

Today's Date:
Prayer Requests and Answers to Prayer

My Thoughts and Praises

> "Therefore I tell you, whatever you ask for in prayer,
> believe that you have received it, and it will be yours."
> MARK 11:24 NIV

Day 106

Today's Date:
Prayer Requests and Answers to Prayer

My Thoughts and Praises

Day 107

Today's Date:
Prayer Requests and Answers to Prayer

My Thoughts and Praises

Day 108

Today's Date:
Prayer Requests and Answers to Prayer

My Thoughts and Praises

Day 109

Today's Date:
Prayer Requests and Answers to Prayer

My Thoughts and Praises

Day 110

Today's Date:
Prayer Requests and Answers to Prayer

My Thoughts and Praises

Day 111

Today's Date:
Prayer Requests and Answers to Prayer

My Thoughts and Praises

> *Certain thoughts are prayers. There are moments when, whatever be the attitude of the body, the soul is on its knees.*
> — Victor Hugo

Day 112

Today's Date:
Prayer Requests and Answers to Prayer

My Thoughts and Praises

Day 113

Today's Date: ....
Prayer Requests and Answers to Prayer ....

My Thoughts and Praises ....

*There is surely a future hope for you,
and your hope will not be cut off.*
PROVERBS 23:18 NIV

Day 114

Today's Date: ....
Prayer Requests and Answers to Prayer ....

My Thoughts and Praises ....

Day 115

Today's Date:
Prayer Requests and Answers to Prayer

My Thoughts and Praises

Day 116

Today's Date:
Prayer Requests and Answers to Prayer

My Thoughts and Praises

Day 117

Today's Date:
Prayer Requests and Answers to Prayer

My Thoughts and Praises

Day 118

Today's Date:
Prayer Requests and Answers to Prayer

My Thoughts and Praises

Day 119

Today's Date:
Prayer Requests and Answers to Prayer

My Thoughts and Praises

> *When you pray, better to have your heart be without words than your words without heart.... The best prayers have often more groans than words.*
> JOHN BUNYAN

Day 120

Today's Date:
Prayer Requests and Answers to Prayer

My Thoughts and Praises

Day 121

Today's Date:
Prayer Requests and Answers to Prayer

My Thoughts and Praises

> *"Yet not my will, but yours be done."*
> Luke 22:42 NIV

Day 122

Today's Date:
Prayer Requests and Answers to Prayer

My Thoughts and Praises

Day 123

Today's Date:
Prayer Requests and Answers to Prayer

My Thoughts and Praises

Day 124

Today's Date:
Prayer Requests and Answers to Prayer

My Thoughts and Praises

Day 125

Today's Date:
Prayer Requests and Answers to Prayer

My Thoughts and Praises

Day 126

Today's Date:
Prayer Requests and Answers to Prayer

My Thoughts and Praises

Day 127

Today's Date:
Prayer Requests and Answers to Prayer

My Thoughts and Praises

> *A man who is intimate with God will never be intimidated by men.*
> LEONARD RAVENHILL

Day 128

Today's Date:
Prayer Requests and Answers to Prayer

My Thoughts and Praises

Day 129

Today's Date:
Prayer Requests and Answers to Prayer

My Thoughts and Praises

> "This, then, is how you should pray:
> 'Our Father in heaven, hallowed be your name.'"
> MATTHEW 6:9 NIV

Day 130

Today's Date:
Prayer Requests and Answers to Prayer

My Thoughts and Praises

Day 131

Today's Date:
Prayer Requests and Answers to Prayer

My Thoughts and Praises

Day 132

Today's Date:
Prayer Requests and Answers to Prayer

My Thoughts and Praises

Day 133

Today's Date:
Prayer Requests and Answers to Prayer

My Thoughts and Praises

Day 134

Today's Date:
Prayer Requests and Answers to Prayer

My Thoughts and Praises

Day 135

Today's Date:
Prayer Requests and Answers to Prayer

My Thoughts and Praises

> *Our prayers lay the track down which God's power can come.
> Like a mighty locomotive, His power is irresistible,
> but it cannot reach us without rails.*
> WATCHMAN NEE

Day 136

Today's Date:
Prayer Requests and Answers to Prayer

My Thoughts and Praises

Day 137

Today's Date:
Prayer Requests and Answers to Prayer

My Thoughts and Praises

> *Do not be anxious about anything,
> but in every situation, by prayer and petition,
> with thanksgiving, present your requests to God.*
> PHILIPPIANS 4:6 NIV

Day 138

Today's Date:
Prayer Requests and Answers to Prayer

My Thoughts and Praises

Day 139

Today's Date:
Prayer Requests and Answers to Prayer

My Thoughts and Praises

Day 140

Today's Date:
Prayer Requests and Answers to Prayer

My Thoughts and Praises

Day 141

Today's Date:
Prayer Requests and Answers to Prayer

My Thoughts and Praises

Day 142

Today's Date:
Prayer Requests and Answers to Prayer

My Thoughts and Praises

Day 143

Today's Date:
Prayer Requests and Answers to Prayer

My Thoughts and Praises

> *Prayer is not monologue, but dialogue.*
> *God's voice in response to mine is its most essential part.*
> ANDREW MURRAY

Day 144

Today's Date:
Prayer Requests and Answers to Prayer

My Thoughts and Praises

Day 145

Today's Date:
Prayer Requests and Answers to Prayer

My Thoughts and Praises

The prayer of a righteous person is powerful and effective.
JAMES 5:16 NIV

Day 146

Today's Date:
Prayer Requests and Answers to Prayer

My Thoughts and Praises

Day 147

Today's Date:

Prayer Requests and Answers to Prayer

My Thoughts and Praises

Day 148

Today's Date:

Prayer Requests and Answers to Prayer

My Thoughts and Praises

Day 149

Today's Date:
Prayer Requests and Answers to Prayer

My Thoughts and Praises

Day 150

Today's Date:
Prayer Requests and Answers to Prayer

My Thoughts and Praises

Day 151

Today's Date:
Prayer Requests and Answers to Prayer

My Thoughts and Praises

Prayer is not learned in a classroom but in the closet.
E. M. BOUNDS

Day 152

Today's Date:
Prayer Requests and Answers to Prayer

My Thoughts and Praises

Day 153

Today's Date:
Prayer Requests and Answers to Prayer

My Thoughts and Praises

> *"Love your enemies and pray for those who persecute you, that you may be children of your Father in heaven."*
> MATTHEW 5:44–45 NIV

Day 154

Today's Date:
Prayer Requests and Answers to Prayer

My Thoughts and Praises

Day 155

Today's Date:
Prayer Requests and Answers to Prayer

My Thoughts and Praises

Day 156

Today's Date:
Prayer Requests and Answers to Prayer

My Thoughts and Praises

Day 157

Today's Date:
Prayer Requests and Answers to Prayer

My Thoughts and Praises

Day 158

Today's Date:
Prayer Requests and Answers to Prayer

My Thoughts and Praises

Day 159

Today's Date:
Prayer Requests and Answers to Prayer

My Thoughts and Praises

> *Listening to God is far more important than giving Him our ideas.*
> FRANK LAUBACH

Day 160

Today's Date:
Prayer Requests and Answers to Prayer

My Thoughts and Praises

Day 161

Today's Date:
Prayer Requests and Answers to Prayer

My Thoughts and Praises

> *If my people, who are called by my name, will humble themselves and pray and seek my face and turn from their wicked ways, then I will hear from heaven, and I will forgive their sin and will heal their land.*
> 2 Chronicles 7:14 NIV

Day 162

Today's Date:
Prayer Requests and Answers to Prayer

My Thoughts and Praises

Day 163

Today's Date:
Prayer Requests and Answers to Prayer

My Thoughts and Praises

Day 164

Today's Date:
Prayer Requests and Answers to Prayer

My Thoughts and Praises

Day 165

Today's Date:
Prayer Requests and Answers to Prayer

My Thoughts and Praises

Day 166

Today's Date:
Prayer Requests and Answers to Prayer

My Thoughts and Praises

Day 167

Today's Date:
Prayer Requests and Answers to Prayer

My Thoughts and Praises

> *It is not enough to begin to pray, nor to pray aright; nor is it enough to continue for a time to pray; but we must patiently, believingly, continue in prayer until we obtain an answer.*
> —George Müller

Day 168

Today's Date:
Prayer Requests and Answers to Prayer

My Thoughts and Praises

Day 169

Today's Date:
Prayer Requests and Answers to Prayer

My Thoughts and Praises

> We constantly pray for you, that our God may make you worthy of his calling, and that by his power he may bring to fruition your every desire for goodness and your every deed prompted by faith.
> 2 Thessalonians 1:11 NIV

Day 170

Today's Date:
Prayer Requests and Answers to Prayer

My Thoughts and Praises

Day 171

Today's Date:
Prayer Requests and Answers to Prayer

My Thoughts and Praises

Day 172

Today's Date:
Prayer Requests and Answers to Prayer

My Thoughts and Praises

Day 173

Today's Date:
Prayer Requests and Answers to Prayer

My Thoughts and Praises

Day 174

Today's Date:
Prayer Requests and Answers to Prayer

My Thoughts and Praises

Day 175

Today's Date:
Prayer Requests and Answers to Prayer

My Thoughts and Praises

Every wish is like a prayer—with God.
ELIZABETH BARRETT BROWNING

Day 176

Today's Date:
Prayer Requests and Answers to Prayer

My Thoughts and Praises

Day 177

Today's Date:
Prayer Requests and Answers to Prayer

My Thoughts and Praises

> *I remember you in my prayers at all times.*
> ROMANS 1:9–10 NIV

Day 178

Today's Date:
Prayer Requests and Answers to Prayer

My Thoughts and Praises

Day 179

Today's Date:
Prayer Requests and Answers to Prayer

My Thoughts and Praises

Day 180

Today's Date:
Prayer Requests and Answers to Prayer

My Thoughts and Praises

Day 181

Today's Date:
Prayer Requests and Answers to Prayer

My Thoughts and Praises

Day 182

Today's Date:
Prayer Requests and Answers to Prayer

My Thoughts and Praises

Day 183

Today's Date:
Prayer Requests and Answers to Prayer

My Thoughts and Praises

> *The word of God is the food by which prayer is nourished and made strong.*
> E. M. BOUNDS

Day 184

Today's Date:
Prayer Requests and Answers to Prayer

My Thoughts and Praises

Day 185

Today's Date:
Prayer Requests and Answers to Prayer

My Thoughts and Praises

"And when you stand praying, if you hold anything against anyone, forgive them, so that your Father in heaven may forgive you your sins."
MARK 11:25 NIV

Day 186

Today's Date:
Prayer Requests and Answers to Prayer

My Thoughts and Praises

Day 187

Today's Date:
Prayer Requests and Answers to Prayer

My Thoughts and Praises

Day 188

Today's Date:
Prayer Requests and Answers to Prayer

My Thoughts and Praises

Day 189

Today's Date:
Prayer Requests and Answers to Prayer

My Thoughts and Praises

Day 190

Today's Date:
Prayer Requests and Answers to Prayer

My Thoughts and Praises

Day 191

Today's Date:
Prayer Requests and Answers to Prayer

My Thoughts and Praises

> *I would rather teach one man to pray than ten men to preach.*
> — CHARLES SPURGEON

Day 192

Today's Date:
Prayer Requests and Answers to Prayer

My Thoughts and Praises

Day 193

Today's Date:
Prayer Requests and Answers to Prayer

My Thoughts and Praises

> *The LORD is all I have, and so in him I put my hope. The LORD is good to everyone who trusts in him.*
> LAMENTATIONS 3:24–25 GNT

Day 194

Today's Date:
Prayer Requests and Answers to Prayer

My Thoughts and Praises

Day 195

Today's Date:
Prayer Requests and Answers to Prayer

My Thoughts and Praises

Day 196

Today's Date:
Prayer Requests and Answers to Prayer

My Thoughts and Praises

Day 197

Today's Date:
Prayer Requests and Answers to Prayer

My Thoughts and Praises

Day 198

Today's Date:
Prayer Requests and Answers to Prayer

My Thoughts and Praises

Day 199

Today's Date:
Prayer Requests and Answers to Prayer

My Thoughts and Praises

The devil. . .trembles when we pray.
SAMUEL CHADWICK

Day 200

Today's Date:
Prayer Requests and Answers to Prayer

My Thoughts and Praises

Day 201

Today's Date:
Prayer Requests and Answers to Prayer

My Thoughts and Praises

*Come near to God and
he will come near to you.*
JAMES 4:8 NIV

Day 202

Today's Date:
Prayer Requests and Answers to Prayer

My Thoughts and Praises

Day 203

Today's Date:
Prayer Requests and Answers to Prayer

My Thoughts and Praises

Day 204

Today's Date:
Prayer Requests and Answers to Prayer

My Thoughts and Praises

Day 205

Today's Date:
Prayer Requests and Answers to Prayer

My Thoughts and Praises

Day 206

Today's Date:
Prayer Requests and Answers to Prayer

My Thoughts and Praises

Day 207

Today's Date:
Prayer Requests and Answers to Prayer

My Thoughts and Praises

> *Prayer is not overcoming God's reluctance,
> but laying hold of His willingness.*
> MARTIN LUTHER

Day 208

Today's Date:
Prayer Requests and Answers to Prayer

My Thoughts and Praises

Day 209

Today's Date:
Prayer Requests and Answers to Prayer

My Thoughts and Praises

Turn your ear to me, come quickly to my rescue; be my rock of refuge, a strong fortress to save me.
PSALM 31:2 NIV

Day 210

Today's Date:
Prayer Requests and Answers to Prayer

My Thoughts and Praises

Day 211

Today's Date:

Prayer Requests and Answers to Prayer

My Thoughts and Praises

Day 212

Today's Date:

Prayer Requests and Answers to Prayer

My Thoughts and Praises

Day 213

Today's Date:
Prayer Requests and Answers to Prayer

My Thoughts and Praises

Day 214

Today's Date:
Prayer Requests and Answers to Prayer

My Thoughts and Praises

Day 215

Today's Date:
Prayer Requests and Answers to Prayer

My Thoughts and Praises

> *[God] is always moving about His work to shape and arrange events in His wise government of our lives.*
> JOHN OF THE CROSS

Day 216

Today's Date:
Prayer Requests and Answers to Prayer

My Thoughts and Praises

Day 217

Today's Date:
Prayer Requests and Answers to Prayer

My Thoughts and Praises

> *Hear my cry, O God; listen to my prayer. From the ends of the earth I call to you, I call as my heart grows faint; lead me to the rock that is higher than I.*
> Psalm 61:1–2 niv

Day 218

Today's Date:
Prayer Requests and Answers to Prayer

My Thoughts and Praises

Day 219

Today's Date:
Prayer Requests and Answers to Prayer

My Thoughts and Praises

Day 220

Today's Date:
Prayer Requests and Answers to Prayer

My Thoughts and Praises

Day 221

Today's Date:
Prayer Requests and Answers to Prayer

My Thoughts and Praises

Day 222

Today's Date:
Prayer Requests and Answers to Prayer

My Thoughts and Praises

Day 223

Today's Date:
Prayer Requests and Answers to Prayer

My Thoughts and Praises

> *When at night you cannot sleep,
> talk to the Shepherd and stop counting sheep.*
> UNKNOWN

Day 224

Today's Date:
Prayer Requests and Answers to Prayer

My Thoughts and Praises

Day 225

Today's Date:
Prayer Requests and Answers to Prayer

My Thoughts and Praises

> *Answer me, LORD, out of the goodness of your love;*
> *in your great mercy turn to me.*
> PSALM 69:16 NIV

Day 226

Today's Date:
Prayer Requests and Answers to Prayer

My Thoughts and Praises

Day 227

Today's Date:
Prayer Requests and Answers to Prayer

My Thoughts and Praises

Day 228

Today's Date:
Prayer Requests and Answers to Prayer

My Thoughts and Praises

Day 229

Today's Date:
Prayer Requests and Answers to Prayer

My Thoughts and Praises

Day 230

Today's Date:
Prayer Requests and Answers to Prayer

My Thoughts and Praises

Day 231

Today's Date:
Prayer Requests and Answers to Prayer

My Thoughts and Praises

> *Look to God and God alone. His strength will help you fly up through the clouds and into His light.*
> VIOLA RUELKE GOMMER

Day 232

Today's Date:
Prayer Requests and Answers to Prayer

My Thoughts and Praises

Day 233

Today's Date:
Prayer Requests and Answers to Prayer

My Thoughts and Praises

> *When you ask, you must believe and not doubt, because the one who doubts is like a wave of the sea, blown and tossed by the wind. That person should not expect to receive anything from the Lord.*
> JAMES 1:6–7 NIV

Day 234

Today's Date:
Prayer Requests and Answers to Prayer

My Thoughts and Praises

Day 235

Today's Date:
Prayer Requests and Answers to Prayer

My Thoughts and Praises

Day 236

Today's Date:
Prayer Requests and Answers to Prayer

My Thoughts and Praises

Day 237

Today's Date:
Prayer Requests and Answers to Prayer

My Thoughts and Praises

Day 238

Today's Date:
Prayer Requests and Answers to Prayer

My Thoughts and Praises

Day 239

Today's Date:

Prayer Requests and Answers to Prayer

My Thoughts and Praises

> *I have been driven many times to my knees by the overwhelming conviction that I had nowhere else to go.*
> ABRAHAM LINCOLN

Day 240

Today's Date:

Prayer Requests and Answers to Prayer

My Thoughts and Praises

Day 241

Today's Date:
Prayer Requests and Answers to Prayer

My Thoughts and Praises

---

*Rejoice in hope,
be patient in suffering, persevere in prayer.*
ROMANS 12:12 NRSV

Day 242

Today's Date:
Prayer Requests and Answers to Prayer

My Thoughts and Praises

Day 243

Today's Date:

Prayer Requests and Answers to Prayer

My Thoughts and Praises

Day 244

Today's Date:

Prayer Requests and Answers to Prayer

My Thoughts and Praises

Day 245

Today's Date:
Prayer Requests and Answers to Prayer

My Thoughts and Praises

Day 246

Today's Date:
Prayer Requests and Answers to Prayer

My Thoughts and Praises

Day 247

Today's Date:
Prayer Requests and Answers to Prayer

My Thoughts and Praises

When we pray, our hearts glow a glorious joy that lights our souls and all the world around us.
TERRI GUILLEMETS

Day 248

Today's Date:
Prayer Requests and Answers to Prayer

My Thoughts and Praises

Day 249

Today's Date:
Prayer Requests and Answers to Prayer

My Thoughts and Praises

> *Ascribe to the LORD the glory due his name;*
> *worship the LORD in the splendor of his holiness.*
> PSALM 29:2 NIV

Day 250

Today's Date:
Prayer Requests and Answers to Prayer

My Thoughts and Praises

Day 251

Today's Date:
Prayer Requests and Answers to Prayer

My Thoughts and Praises

Day 252

Today's Date:
Prayer Requests and Answers to Prayer

My Thoughts and Praises

Day 253

Today's Date:
Prayer Requests and Answers to Prayer

My Thoughts and Praises

Day 254

Today's Date:
Prayer Requests and Answers to Prayer

My Thoughts and Praises

Day 255

Today's Date:
Prayer Requests and Answers to Prayer

My Thoughts and Praises

> *God speaks in the silence of the heart.*
> *Listening is the beginning of prayer.*
> MOTHER TERESA

Day 256

Today's Date:
Prayer Requests and Answers to Prayer

My Thoughts and Praises

Day 257

Today's Date:
Prayer Requests and Answers to Prayer

My Thoughts and Praises

> *The LORD is my shepherd, I lack nothing.*
> *He makes me lie down in green pastures, he leads*
> *me beside quiet waters, he refreshes my soul.*
> PSALM 23:1–2 NIV

Day 258

Today's Date:
Prayer Requests and Answers to Prayer

My Thoughts and Praises

Day 259

Today's Date:
Prayer Requests and Answers to Prayer

My Thoughts and Praises

Day 260

Today's Date:
Prayer Requests and Answers to Prayer

My Thoughts and Praises

Day 261

Today's Date:
Prayer Requests and Answers to Prayer

My Thoughts and Praises

Day 262

Today's Date:
Prayer Requests and Answers to Prayer

My Thoughts and Praises

Day 263

Today's Date:
Prayer Requests and Answers to Prayer

My Thoughts and Praises

> *Prayer is a force as real as terrestrial gravity. It supplies us with a flow of sustaining power in our daily lives.*
> ALEXIS CARREL

Day 264

Today's Date:
Prayer Requests and Answers to Prayer

My Thoughts and Praises

Day 265

Today's Date:
Prayer Requests and Answers to Prayer

My Thoughts and Praises

> *You, Lord, are my lamp; the Lord turns my darkness into light. With your help I can advance against a troop; with my God I can scale a wall.*
> 2 Samuel 22:29–30 niv

Day 266

Today's Date:
Prayer Requests and Answers to Prayer

My Thoughts and Praises

Day 267

Today's Date:
Prayer Requests and Answers to Prayer

My Thoughts and Praises

Day 268

Today's Date:
Prayer Requests and Answers to Prayer

My Thoughts and Praises

Day 269

Today's Date:
Prayer Requests and Answers to Prayer

My Thoughts and Praises

Day 270

Today's Date:
Prayer Requests and Answers to Prayer

My Thoughts and Praises

Day 271

Today's Date:
Prayer Requests and Answers to Prayer

My Thoughts and Praises

> *God always answers our prayers,
> but sometimes the answer is no.*
> UNKNOWN

Day 272

Today's Date:
Prayer Requests and Answers to Prayer

My Thoughts and Praises

Day 273

Today's Date:
Prayer Requests and Answers to Prayer

My Thoughts and Praises

*Because of the LORD's great love we are not consumed,
for his compassions never fail. They are new
every morning; great is your faithfulness.*
LAMENTATIONS 3:22–23 NIV

Day 274

Today's Date:
Prayer Requests and Answers to Prayer

My Thoughts and Praises

Day 275

Today's Date:
Prayer Requests and Answers to Prayer

My Thoughts and Praises

Day 276

Today's Date:
Prayer Requests and Answers to Prayer

My Thoughts and Praises

Day 277

Today's Date:
Prayer Requests and Answers to Prayer

My Thoughts and Praises

Day 278

Today's Date:
Prayer Requests and Answers to Prayer

My Thoughts and Praises

Day 279

Today's Date:
Prayer Requests and Answers to Prayer

My Thoughts and Praises

*When prayers go up,
blessings come down.*
UNKNOWN

Day 280

Today's Date:
Prayer Requests and Answers to Prayer

My Thoughts and Praises

Day 281

Today's Date:
Prayer Requests and Answers to Prayer

My Thoughts and Praises

> *I have obeyed the* L*ord* *my God. . . . Now look down from your holy dwelling place in heaven and bless your people.*
> D*euteronomy* 26:14–15 nlt

Day 282

Today's Date:
Prayer Requests and Answers to Prayer

My Thoughts and Praises

Day 283

Today's Date:
Prayer Requests and Answers to Prayer

My Thoughts and Praises

Day 284

Today's Date:
Prayer Requests and Answers to Prayer

My Thoughts and Praises

Day 285

Today's Date:
Prayer Requests and Answers to Prayer

My Thoughts and Praises

Day 286

Today's Date:
Prayer Requests and Answers to Prayer

My Thoughts and Praises

Day 287

Today's Date:
Prayer Requests and Answers to Prayer

My Thoughts and Praises

---

*Our prayers should be for blessings in general,
for God knows best what is good for us.*
SOCRATES

Day 288

Today's Date:
Prayer Requests and Answers to Prayer

My Thoughts and Praises

Day 289

Today's Date:
Prayer Requests and Answers to Prayer

My Thoughts and Praises

*Find rest in God; my hope comes from him.
Truly he is my rock and my salvation;
he is my fortress, I will not be shaken.*
PSALM 62:5–6 NIV

Day 290

Today's Date:
Prayer Requests and Answers to Prayer

My Thoughts and Praises

Day 291

Today's Date:
Prayer Requests and Answers to Prayer

My Thoughts and Praises

Day 292

Today's Date:
Prayer Requests and Answers to Prayer

My Thoughts and Praises

Day 293

Today's Date:
Prayer Requests and Answers to Prayer

My Thoughts and Praises

Day 294

Today's Date:
Prayer Requests and Answers to Prayer

My Thoughts and Praises

Day 295

Today's Date:
Prayer Requests and Answers to Prayer

My Thoughts and Praises

The simple heart that freely asks in love, obtains.
JOHN GREENLEAF WHITTIER

Day 296

Today's Date:
Prayer Requests and Answers to Prayer

My Thoughts and Praises

Day 297

Today's Date:
Prayer Requests and Answers to Prayer

My Thoughts and Praises

> *Hear my voice in accordance with your love;*
> *preserve my life, Lord, according to your laws.*
> Psalm 119:149 niv

Day 298

Today's Date:
Prayer Requests and Answers to Prayer

My Thoughts and Praises

Day 299

Today's Date:
Prayer Requests and Answers to Prayer

My Thoughts and Praises

Day 300

Today's Date:
Prayer Requests and Answers to Prayer

My Thoughts and Praises

Day 301

Today's Date:
Prayer Requests and Answers to Prayer

My Thoughts and Praises

Day 302

Today's Date:
Prayer Requests and Answers to Prayer

My Thoughts and Praises

Day 303

Today's Date:
Prayer Requests and Answers to Prayer

My Thoughts and Praises

> *I'm glad that God knows my heart; His Spirit moves through my concern and turns it into prayer.*
> ELLYN SANNA

Day 304

Today's Date:
Prayer Requests and Answers to Prayer

My Thoughts and Praises

Day 305

Today's Date:
Prayer Requests and Answers to Prayer

My Thoughts and Praises

> *Send me your light and your faithful care, let them lead me; let them bring me to your holy mountain, to the place where you dwell.*
> Psalm 43:3 niv

Day 306

Today's Date:
Prayer Requests and Answers to Prayer

My Thoughts and Praises

Day 307

Today's Date:

Prayer Requests and Answers to Prayer

My Thoughts and Praises

Day 308

Today's Date:

Prayer Requests and Answers to Prayer

My Thoughts and Praises

Day 309

Today's Date:

Prayer Requests and Answers to Prayer

My Thoughts and Praises

Day 310

Today's Date:

Prayer Requests and Answers to Prayer

My Thoughts and Praises

Day 311

Today's Date:
Prayer Requests and Answers to Prayer

My Thoughts and Praises

> *Be thankful that God's answers are wiser than your answers.*
> — WILLIAM CULBERTSON

Day 312

Today's Date:
Prayer Requests and Answers to Prayer

My Thoughts and Praises

Day 313

Today's Date:

Prayer Requests and Answers to Prayer

My Thoughts and Praises

> *The eternal God is your refuge,
> and underneath are the everlasting arms.*
> DEUTERONOMY 33:27 NIV

Day 314

Today's Date:

Prayer Requests and Answers to Prayer

My Thoughts and Praises

Day 315

Today's Date:
Prayer Requests and Answers to Prayer

My Thoughts and Praises

Day 316

Today's Date:
Prayer Requests and Answers to Prayer

My Thoughts and Praises

Day 317

Today's Date:
Prayer Requests and Answers to Prayer

My Thoughts and Praises

Day 318

Today's Date:
Prayer Requests and Answers to Prayer

My Thoughts and Praises

Day 319

Today's Date:
Prayer Requests and Answers to Prayer

My Thoughts and Praises

> *Don't be afraid to desire great mercies from the God of heaven.*
> JOHN BUNYAN

Day 320

Today's Date:
Prayer Requests and Answers to Prayer

My Thoughts and Praises

Day 321

Today's Date:
Prayer Requests and Answers to Prayer

My Thoughts and Praises

*Be strong and let your heart take courage,
all you who hope in the Lord.*
Psalm 31:24 nasb

Day 322

Today's Date:
Prayer Requests and Answers to Prayer

My Thoughts and Praises

Day 323

Today's Date:
Prayer Requests and Answers to Prayer

My Thoughts and Praises

Day 324

Today's Date:
Prayer Requests and Answers to Prayer

My Thoughts and Praises

Day 325

Today's Date:
Prayer Requests and Answers to Prayer

My Thoughts and Praises

Day 326

Today's Date:
Prayer Requests and Answers to Prayer

My Thoughts and Praises

Day 327

Today's Date:
Prayer Requests and Answers to Prayer

My Thoughts and Praises

> *We must move from asking God to take care of the things that are breaking our hearts, to praying about the things that are breaking His heart.*
> M. Gibb

Day 328

Today's Date:
Prayer Requests and Answers to Prayer

My Thoughts and Praises

Day 329

Today's Date:
Prayer Requests and Answers to Prayer

My Thoughts and Praises

> *When I am afraid, I put my trust in you.*
> PSALM 56:3 NIV

Day 330

Today's Date:
Prayer Requests and Answers to Prayer

My Thoughts and Praises

Day 331

Today's Date:
Prayer Requests and Answers to Prayer

My Thoughts and Praises

Day 332

Today's Date:
Prayer Requests and Answers to Prayer

My Thoughts and Praises

Day 333

Today's Date:
Prayer Requests and Answers to Prayer

My Thoughts and Praises

Day 334

Today's Date:
Prayer Requests and Answers to Prayer

My Thoughts and Praises

Day 335

Today's Date:
Prayer Requests and Answers to Prayer

My Thoughts and Praises

*The deepest wishes of the heart
find expression in secret prayer.*
GEORGE E. REES

Day 336

Today's Date:
Prayer Requests and Answers to Prayer

My Thoughts and Praises

Day 337

Today's Date:
Prayer Requests and Answers to Prayer

My Thoughts and Praises

> *Pray all the time; thank God no matter what happens. This is the way God wants you who belong to Christ Jesus to live.*
> 1 THESSALONIANS 5:17–18 MSG

Day 338

Today's Date:
Prayer Requests and Answers to Prayer

My Thoughts and Praises

Day 339

Today's Date:
Prayer Requests and Answers to Prayer

My Thoughts and Praises

Day 340

Today's Date:
Prayer Requests and Answers to Prayer

My Thoughts and Praises

Day 341

Today's Date:
Prayer Requests and Answers to Prayer

My Thoughts and Praises

Day 342

Today's Date:
Prayer Requests and Answers to Prayer

My Thoughts and Praises

Day 343

Today's Date:
Prayer Requests and Answers to Prayer

My Thoughts and Praises

[Prayer is] the best way we have to draw strength from heaven.
J. BAKER

Day 344

Today's Date:
Prayer Requests and Answers to Prayer

My Thoughts and Praises

Day 345

Today's Date:
Prayer Requests and Answers to Prayer

My Thoughts and Praises

> *I can do everything through Christ,
> who gives me strength.*
> PHILIPPIANS 4:13 NLT

Day 346

Today's Date:
Prayer Requests and Answers to Prayer

My Thoughts and Praises

Day 347

Today's Date:
Prayer Requests and Answers to Prayer

My Thoughts and Praises

Day 348

Today's Date:
Prayer Requests and Answers to Prayer

My Thoughts and Praises

Day 349

Today's Date:
Prayer Requests and Answers to Prayer

My Thoughts and Praises

Day 350

Today's Date:
Prayer Requests and Answers to Prayer

My Thoughts and Praises

Day 351

Today's Date:
Prayer Requests and Answers to Prayer

My Thoughts and Praises

> *Some have been to the mountain.*
> *I have been to my knees by the side of my bed.*
> ROBERT BRAULT

Day 352

Today's Date:
Prayer Requests and Answers to Prayer

My Thoughts and Praises

Day 353

Today's Date:
Prayer Requests and Answers to Prayer

My Thoughts and Praises

> *God assured us, "I'll never let you down, never walk off and leave you."*
> HEBREWS 13:5 MSG

Day 354

Today's Date:
Prayer Requests and Answers to Prayer

My Thoughts and Praises

Day 355

Today's Date:
Prayer Requests and Answers to Prayer

My Thoughts and Praises

Day 356

Today's Date:
Prayer Requests and Answers to Prayer

My Thoughts and Praises

Day 357

Today's Date:
Prayer Requests and Answers to Prayer

My Thoughts and Praises

Day 358

Today's Date:
Prayer Requests and Answers to Prayer

My Thoughts and Praises

Day 359

Today's Date:
Prayer Requests and Answers to Prayer

My Thoughts and Praises

> *Prayers not felt by us are seldom heard by God.*
> PHILIP HENRY

Day 360

Today's Date:
Prayer Requests and Answers to Prayer

My Thoughts and Praises

Day 361

Today's Date:
Prayer Requests and Answers to Prayer

My Thoughts and Praises

> *The Lord is trustworthy in all he promises and faithful in all he does.*
> Psalm 145:13 niv

Day 362

Today's Date:
Prayer Requests and Answers to Prayer

My Thoughts and Praises

Day 363

Today's Date:
Prayer Requests and Answers to Prayer

My Thoughts and Praises

Day 364

Today's Date:
Prayer Requests and Answers to Prayer

My Thoughts and Praises

Day 365

Today's Date:

Prayer Requests and Answers to Prayer

My Thoughts and Praises

God grant me the serenity to accept the things I cannot change, courage to change the things I can, and the wisdom to know the difference.
REINHOLD NIEBUHR

Notes

Notes

Notes

Notes